I Am Alone: What Next?

A story of learning and relearning about loss and gain

By
Lady Edith Ebohon

Copyright © 2025 Lady Edith Ebohon

ISBN: 978-1-917601-57-3

Unless otherwise indicated, Scripture quotations are taken from The Holy Bible, New International Version (Anglicized edition). Copyright © 1979, 1984, 2011 by Biblica. Used by permission of Hodder & Stoughton Ltd, an Hachette UK company. All rights reserved. 'NIV' is a registered trademark of Biblica. UK trademark number 1448790.

Scripture quotations marked NIV 1984 are taken from the HOLY BIBLE, NEW INTERNATIONAL VERSION. Copyright © 1973, 1978, 1984 by International Bible Society. Used by permission of Hodder & Stoughton Publishers, a member of the Hachette UK Group. All rights reserved. 'NIV' is a registered trademark of International Bible Society. UK trademark number 1448790.

Scripture quotations marked NLT are taken from the *Holy Bible*, New Living Translation, copyright © 1996, 2004, 2015 by Tyndale House Foundation. Used by permission of Tyndale House Publishers, Inc., Carol Stream, Illinois 60188, USA. All rights reserved.

#hiddeninchrist
#changethestory
#savedbygrace

Dedication

To all people who have been left alone.

I wrote this book, using my lived experience of being alone, and telling how GOD saved and helped me, to help someone out there.

If you gain just one tip (or two), I am grateful to God.

My anchor scripture throughout my difficult days, which I prayed with regularly, was the story of the angels leading Peter out of jail, by the power of the Holy Spirit (Acts 12:6–19). I encourage you to read this.

It helped me to know and feel secure in the power of the HOLY SPIRIT; that there is just nothing GOD cannot do.

I wrote poems, when left alone, and I have included one before each chapter.

Enjoy reading my poems and chapters. I hope you gain one thing or another . . .

About Lady Edith Ebohon

Lady Edith Ebohon is a remarkable woman: a beacon of compassion and inspiration; she has had an extraordinary life, and is a multifaceted individual who wears many hats, with grace and purpose.

By day, Lady Edith is an occupational therapist, dedicating her expertise to the realm of mental health. Through her unwavering commitment and compassionate care, she touches the lives of those battling inner demons, helping them to find the strength to reclaim their lives. Her innovative approach combines the knowledge she has gained from her two degrees in occupational therapy and business administration with marketing, and a master's degree in leadership, which enables her to bridge the gap between health care and effective leadership.

Beyond her professional achievements, Lady Edith's fervent spirit extends to her involvement in charity work. With boundless love for her community, she tirelessly advocates for mental-health awareness and the importance of nurturing positive well-being. Her infectious enthusiasm and unwavering belief in the power of empathy touch the hearts of everyone she encounters.

But Lady Edith's story doesn't end there. She is also a dedicated church worker who finds solace and spiritual fulfilment in her faith. Guided by her unwavering devotion, she uplifts others through her tireless efforts, spreading love and kindness throughout her congregation.

Despite her numerous roles, Lady Edith remains a loving wife, a nurturing mother, and a doting grandmother. With a heart full of love, she effortlessly balances the demands of her family and her career, infusing every aspect of her life with unwavering positive vibes and energy.

Lady Edith loves to use storytelling from aspects of her life – through many trials and triumphs, and about numerous people she has encountered – to inspire others to embrace their own capacity for healing and empowerment, and to make a meaningful difference in their lives. Her own personal story serves as a testimony to the indomitable spirit within each of us and is a reminder that, through love, empathy, and positive energy, we can create a brighter, more compassionate world.

Lady Edith believes that the best way to move forwards in life is to discover the transformative power of faith and God's love in overcoming life's challenges. In a world filled with obstacles and uncertainties, one must cultivate a deep relationship with God. Through prayer, Scripture, and trust in his divine plan, individuals can find solace, guidance, and strength. When surrounded by a supportive Christian community, they can draw on the wisdom of the Bible, seeking encouragement and finding comfort in God's promises. With patience, perseverance, and gratitude, they can embrace the peace that surpasses understanding, knowing that God is ever present, offering the courage and resilience needed to triumph over life's trials. They can unleash the potential within by harnessing the power of faith to navigate life's challenges, with unwavering hope.

Lady Edith is the author of the motivational book *Life's Golden Gems*, as well as a host of the award-winning YouTube shows, *Two Minutes Sunday* and *Relationship Tips, Talks and Tales*. She is a multifaceted speaker and media personality, and is passionate about mental health and issues facing women and vulnerable people. She is available for speaking events all over the world.

Acknowledgements

God
Partner, children, and grandchildren
Family
Church
Fellowships
Friends
All lovers of God and his kingdom

Foreword

This is a well-written book by Edith, which asks the million-dollar question a lot of people are asking at the moment. I always say to people that, in Genesis 2:18: 'The LORD God said, "It is not good for the man to be alone. I will make a helper suitable for him."' God was right then and God is still right now! Unfortunately, the social-media age, particularly the habit of scrolling through a phone, has given everyone a sense of having people around them all the time; but the reality is that it gives a false sense of belonging because, no matter how much AI we see, it is not the same as being with humans. We were created to need each other!

I cried while reading this book, and I am not one who easily cries like that! I cried partly because it woke in me a deep sense of empathy for Edith and the many other women out there dealing with loneliness as a result of being left alone, often suddenly, by loved ones, through divorce, death or disappointment. It also made me cry because I can relate to some of the points she wrote about.

I particularly enjoyed the poetry in each chapter and the use of Bible passages to emphasise her points. I love how Edith doesn't just tell a story, but also provides a solution based on her own experiences.

Her recommendations for therapy are noteworthy because some communities, especially Christian ones, still trivialise the importance of therapy for those experiencing any major life changes or challenges. It teaches us to stay positive, be present with our emotions, be prompt in seeking counselling, and to follow due process rather than fast tracking it.

This book will make you cry and fill your heart with hope at the same time. It should also encourage you to check in regularly with people when their loved ones leave them for whatever reason.

I recommend this book to anyone who is going through a season of change in their life. Embrace the change, get your survival toolkit to navigate the journey, and celebrate the new you. The reality and truth are that, when it feels like everyone has left you, there is a constant friend whose name is EMMANUEL, who never leaves nor forsakes us. Edith's relationship with Emmanuel has been her major inspiration and she invites us all to do the same. Emmanuel wants to instruct you and lead you on the way to go. A rebound-type of relationship only causes more pain, as Edith narrates!

Are you asking yourself right now, 'I am alone: what next?' Well, this book offers you the answer and some guidance.

Thank you, Edith, for your vulnerability, your authenticity, and your honesty. Truly you are a great student of YouNiversity!

Rev. Victoria Lawrence,
CEO, The Father's Joy

Contents

Introduction

Poem 1: Give and take
Chapter One: I am alone: what next?

Poem 2: I have learnt that people who can make you laugh can also make you cry
Chapter Two: Time to forge ahead

Poem 3: I am a WOW woman
Chapter Three: Know yourself

Poem 4: Delete
Chapter Four: Dealing with losses

Poem 5: Life is one big fight
Chapter Five: Support

Poem 6: The scars
Chapter Six: Mood pickers

Poem 7: My identity in Christ
Chapter Seven: Find your purpose

Poem 8: I have let go . . .
Chapter Eight: King and queen

Poem 9: My happiness
Chapter Nine: Finding love again

Closing remarks

Introduction

Being left alone is something no one wants to experience, but it can happen. This book is about being left alone when a marriage and/or a relationship ends due to death, divorce, or separation. This has happened to me on more than one occasion, and I wanted to put this experience in a book to help others. I am not saying that what I suggest here is a solution for everyone, but I am sure you can learn one or two things you can use to help others.

I want to start by saying that being alone is not the same as loneliness, although these are related concepts. Being alone refers to a physical state of being by oneself, often without the presence of others: it is a situation where a person is not in the company of other individuals. Being alone can be a deliberate choice, when someone seeks solitude or personal time. It doesn't necessarily imply negative emotions or a sense of isolation.

Loneliness, on the other hand, is an emotional state characterised by a sense of isolation, disconnection, and sadness. It is a subjective feeling of being socially or emotionally isolated, even when surrounded by others. Loneliness can occur when someone desires more meaningful connections or feels a lack of understanding or companionship.

What strikes me about being alone is that it can be a deliberate choice. The issue is, however, that when it is not deliberate – and someone you love, who has been with you for a while, leaves – it will hurt, especially when you are not expecting to be left alone. Most times, the individual has no plans for what to do when left alone.

For me, my own experience was that it was unexpected;

it was painful;
I was lost.

At this point, it is best to understand that once you are left alone, it is the start of another journey, a new season. For me, it was time to pull up my sleeves and go to work. It was sad, because feelings of previous times when I was left alone all came rushing back to my mind. I had been left alone as a teenager in the diaspora, with no immediate family members; as a widow, after getting married to a complete gentleman and bearing two kids; and when my father passed, when my mother passed, and when loved ones and close friends passed. But I survived. I made it through. However, I did not think I could cope this time around. I had just been left alone again . . . I felt I should end my life. My emotions were too many to deal with. I was overwhelmed, disappointed; I felt shame, raw pain, and guilt. I could not bring my emotions together.

I think this resulted in my thinking and asking so many questions: 'Why me? How? What did I do wrong? Am I not a good person? What could I have done better?' and so on. As a Christian, I did not understand. I realised that I had suddenly lost my main role in life: being a wife. I also realised that I no longer knew who I was: I had lost my identity and the reason my Creator made me, or so I thought. Overwhelming feelings of darkness and sorrow engulfed my entire being. I would sit in darkness for hours on end, with different thoughts, no answers, no hugs, no cuddles, wondering where he was, what he was doing, and stuff like that.

One thing I knew, though, was that I had to rise above this situation and take charge of my life: after all, the Bible told me that God had given me dominion and authority. I started to imagine women in the Bible who had gone through so much, and how they managed to end up in victory: this challenged and motivated me. I had to go back to the loving arms of my maker, my God, my Creator: the one who made me and called me. God is loving, compassionate, and faithful. For me, his child, he is my source of guidance, support, joy, and strength.

Sometimes, difficulties and hardships, such as I was going through then, can be part of a larger plan that we may not fully understand in the present moment. It is during these times that faith, trust, and patience become important.

I felt that I needed to be in touch with my emotions; I needed to face that moment to heal. I felt a sense of sadness, isolation, and emptiness; I felt vulnerable and exposed. At that time, I was not thinking that there might be something positive in this situation, such as being independent and free, with time to have my own personal space; engage in introspection; study myself to find out who I was again; enjoy activities; live my life on my own terms; and consider my happiness, one hundred per cent, without regret or remorse. I did a lot of reflecting and self-examining. It allowed me to delve into my thoughts, explore my emotions, and gain insights about myself. It meant that I could empower myself and be self-reliant.

Poem 1
Give and take

Give and take: everyone is out here for themselves!
They take all they need from you and then they go.
But I can never let them feel like they are above me.
In life, people look out for themselves.
It comes to a time, sometimes, when what they want is not
want you want, and you begin to have differences.
It is painful because you thought the love is for ever but, no,
not so.
They left.
Because it's about them, not you.

Chapter One

I am alone: what next?

These were the questions I asked myself soon after I was left alone: 'I am alone: what next? What am I supposed to do next? What is my next step?' I sat down and I wrote a survival plan on how to recover and heal. I like writing and I like talking, so that was my default mode setting in – but it helped. I recorded my thoughts either by making a voice memo on my phone or by writing in my notebook. I started, on a blank piece of paper, by noting: I AM ALONE: WHAT NEXT?

The first thing that came into my mind was that I needed help: I couldn't help myself. Who better to go to than God Almighty? I needed the higher power of the Holy Spirit. I needed a friend to talk to, and that talking had to be able to be done at any time. I needed someone to talk to; and, trust me, no human can give you that time. The only friend closer than your skin is Jesus, so I decided there and then to make him my best friend.

After all I had no other choice.
God owns the blueprint and the road map to my life.
He made me, and he knew why he made me.
He knew a day like this would happen.

He alone can give one the strategy and light for a suddenly dark world.

I found out that making this decision helped me to talk to Jesus, my Lord and Saviour, at any time, day or night, without an appointment, without letting him know first that

I needed to speak to him. This was amazing; I had so much relief. The other thing about making Jesus my best friend was that I did not have to feel guilty or ashamed, or always try to explain or defend myself. I just simply had to talk to him by pouring out my heart, without fear of being judged. Having Jesus as my best friend was a delightful and fulfilling experience.

The next step was to pray. I know it sounds like, 'Well, we all pray.' But for me, this prayer was more intentional, and it was different from the times I talked to Jesus as my best friend. This was about searching for scriptures on what I was going through, what I was feeling, and using these scriptures to pray.

For example, on a day I felt angry, I would look for verses about anger. I would use these scriptures:

'"In your anger do not sin": do not let the sun go down while you are still angry, and do not give the devil a foothold.' (Ephesians 4:26–27)

'A fool gives full vent to his anger, but a wise man keeps himself under control.' (Proverbs 29:11, NIV 1984)

'Refrain from anger and turn from wrath; do not fret – it leads only to evil.' (Psalm 37:8)

'But I tell you that anyone who is angry with a brother or sister will be subject to judgment.' (Matthew 5:22)

If I was feeling low, I would pray with the following:

'Why are you downcast, O my soul? Why so disturbed within me? Put your hope in God, for I will yet praise him, my Saviour and my God.' (Psalm 42:5, NIV 1984)

'The LORD is close to the broken-hearted and saves those who are crushed in spirit.' (Psalm 34:18)

'Cast all your anxiety on him because he cares for you.' (1 Peter 5:7)

'Do not be anxious about anything, but in every situation, by prayer and petition, with thanksgiving, present your requests to God. And the peace of God, which transcends all understanding, will guard your hearts and your minds in Christ Jesus.' (Philippians 4:6–7)

'Come to me, all you who are weary and burdened, and I will give you rest. Take my yoke upon you and learn from me, for I am gentle and humble in heart, and you will find rest for your souls.' (Matthew 11:28–29)

These verses remind us that we are not alone in our struggles and that God is there to comfort and support us. We can find hope and peace in him, and trust that he will help us through our difficulties.

If I was feeling lonely and alone:

'Be strong and courageous. Do not be afraid or terrified because of them, for the LORD your God goes with you; he will never leave you nor forsake you.' (Deuteronomy 31:6)

'The LORD himself goes before you and will be with you; he will never leave you nor forsake you. Do not be afraid; do not be discouraged.' (Deuteronomy 31:8)

'God is our refuge and strength, an ever-present help in trouble.' (Psalm 46:1)

'The LORD is near to all who call on him, to all who call on him in truth.' (Psalm 145:18)

'Even though I walk through the darkest valley, I will fear no evil, for you are with me; your rod and your staff, they comfort me.' (Psalm 23:4)

These exercises enabled me to gain courage and confidence, and I realised that God loves me just as I am. And they led me to the next step.

The next step was the great realisation that I did not fully comprehend what God had made me for. I had a sudden deep desire to know what God created me for. I once made a *Two Minutes Sunday* video clip (which you can find on YouTube) when I said God did not have time to make a nobody. So here, I asked, 'Am I a nobody?' The answer was 'No!'. I was not created just to be a wife and mother; there was surely more to me. I will talk about this later in the book.

It is very hard to find oneself alone suddenly, and I cannot overemphasise that.

These measures were instrumental in my ability to move on.

Recognising -

Recognising that the individual is no longer a part of your existence. Always take the view that the person will not return, even though it is possible; however, if they do not, you will waste your life and precious time on this hope that may never come true. Wishful thinking only provides a transient sense of optimism and hope. There are risks associated with relying solely on wishful thinking as a coping mechanism or decision-making strategy. Often, wishful thinking involves imagining idealised or implausible scenarios. This can result in setting exaggerated expectations for us or others, which can lead to disappointment and frustration when our desires are not met.

Realising -

Realising that wishful thinking can lead to ignoring or denying facts or evidence that contradict one's desires. This can result in a distorted perception of reality and prevent the individual from confronting and addressing actual problems or challenges. Without taking concrete steps or actions, relying solely on optimistic thinking can result in passivity and a lack of personal agency. Rather than actively working towards goals or solving problems, individuals may passively wait for desired outcomes to materialise, which frequently results in minimal or no progress. It makes you miss opportunities, miss fun, miss new ideas.

I want you to know that many people get stuck in this phase of wishful thinking after a relationship ends. It has more negative impacts than positive; it can affect your mental health when you eventually learn that the person is no longer coming back, and that you have wasted so much time.

<u>Seeking -</u>
Seeking support from friends can be very helpful for your mental and emotional well-being. Friends can provide you with a sense of comfort, understanding, and encouragement during difficult times. They can also offer different perspectives on your problems and provide practical advice on how to address them.

<u>Try not to -</u>
Trying not to talk to the person that left. Try not to think about what they are doing; try not to ask others about them; and try not to check their status and all their social media pages. Continually thinking about the person can be damaging and stop you from healing and moving on. Rather, find ways to redirect your thoughts and focus on positive things in your life. Distract yourself from making the person the central focus of your mind.

<u>Crying –</u>
Cry, if you must, it is ok to cry: it is an expression of how you are feeling, and sometimes provides some relief. Crying is natural and we as humans will cry in response to pain we feel – mentally, physically or otherwise. When we cry, it helps us to regulate our emotions; it can also provide relief. Sometimes bottling up emotions is more detrimental to us than necessary. So, if you feel like crying, do so; let your emotions out. It is normal and healthy. Crying can be a helpful way to navigate and process your emotions.

<u>Take care of you -</u>
Taking care of yourself: try to eat, drink, go out, and do things you enjoy. Exercise, sleep and such self-care things aid in the healing process. Do things for fun; be intentional about your self-care. Try also to do things you have always wanted to do but put off. Try new things you have never done.

Poem 2

I have learnt that people who can make you laugh can also make you cry

Life is sad!
Life is happy!
Whatever the case, I have God.
I will not allow any more sadness, starting from here, from now.
I am not going to let what someone else does or does not do determine the type of person I am called to be.
I will not allow them to make me cry just because they can make me happy.
I refuse to put my trust in things that do not matter or in things that do not build me up,
such as
malice,
unforgiveness,
bitterness,
worldly wealth,
gossip.
I will put my trust in God Almighty.

By doing this, I will be letting go of the good to grab hold of better, the best, and excellence.

Chapter Two

Time to forge ahead

Remember there is a long road ahead in recovery, and recovery time is different for each person. The longer you were with the person that left, the harder and more difficult the road to healing will be. This is because they left you: you never wanted to leave, so you did not have a plan.

But guess what? Talk to yourself and, if possible, shout it out loud: call your name and say, 'It is my time to come alive. It is time to move on. It is time to forge ahead.'

Start today – right now. Decide to recover. No matter what it takes, make a determined, conscious, deliberate, intentional decision to move on.

Start by forgiving yourself and forgiving them.

Do not blame them and do not blame yourself!

I give the next step with caution, as it might not be for everyone, but what I did was to delete pictures of him and of us from my phone. I also removed pictures in the house of us or of him. This is because it helped me to think about me and my children, and what I needed next in my life. This was a hard exercise to conduct because it did not make the pain of his leaving go away, but I did it to reduce the memories of us. Remembering all the time and investment in the relationship will hurt, but this must be dealt with.

Another thing that helped in forging ahead was to have no contact with him. Do not contact them and do not let them contact you. You need to heal emotionally, psychologically, physically, and spiritually so you can move on. Be ready to deal with the pain and the hurt. You will miss the person; you will want to be with them, talk to them, hold them, and ask them questions to get more understanding about what happened; but you must be strong and let go. You must embrace this part of your journey; it is a journey – a very long one.

Focus on your result and why you are doing this, because you need to be sane to be alive. Break the power/control/influence they have over you. You will have days and moments when you will have emotions and thoughts such as

fear: 'Will I be alone for ever?'
shame: 'What will people say?'
guilt: 'Should I have done this or that differently?'
assumptions: 'They never loved me; they used me.'
wrong conclusions: 'All men are dogs', 'All women are liars', 'Marriage is not for me. Marriage is a scam.'

The way to deal with these emotions and thoughts will become more evident to you as you read along.

An explanation of Acts 12:6–19 and how it helped me.
Here is what I learned from this passage.

God's intervention: the narrative emphasises God's power and intervention in his followers' lives. Despite Peter's incarceration and looming trial, God miraculously released him, proving his ability to transcend any human restriction or hindrance.

The power of prayer: the early Christians prayed passionately for Peter's release, and their prayers were rewarded. This chapter emphasises the significance and usefulness of prayer in seeking God's involvement and assistance in tough situations.

God's sovereignty: even in the face of persecution and danger, the scripture reminds us that God is in control.

Despite King Herod's preparations and the obstacles Peter encountered, God's plan prevailed, and Peter was delivered.

The role of faith: Peter's reaction to the angel's instructions, as well as his subsequent acts, necessitated trust and obedience. Even when faced with uncertainty and probable danger, his faith in God's rescue drove him to follow the angel's counsel.

Overall, Acts 12:6–19, teaches us about the power of God, the significance of prayer, God's sovereignty over earthly rulers, and the significance of faith and obedience in difficult circumstances.

Poem 3

I am a WOW woman

What does WOW mean?

WOW means

- *to express astonishment or admiration for something or someone;*
- *when something is a sensational success;*
- *to impress and excite (someone) greatly.*

A WOW woman is a woman who, when people see her, they admire her because they see something sensational in her. They hear her success story; they feel impressed and astonished by her.

I am a WOW woman.
I say that I am a WOW woman because that is what I want to be, and I see myself there now, even though I am not there yet.
I am working towards becoming a woman of whom, when people see and hear my story, they will say, 'She is a WOW woman.'
They will know that God has been faithful to me.

#wowwoman
#womanofwisdom
#womanofworship
#womanofwinnings
#womanofwonder
#womanofwealth

Chapter Three

Know yourself

One big element for me, as I was healing, was that I realised that I did not know who I was any more. Who was I really? A wife, a mother, a church leader/worker, an occupational therapist? I asked, 'Who exactly am I? How do I define myself?' I grasped that I had been so focused on playing the role of a wife and mother that I did not even know what I liked, enjoyed, or wanted for myself any more. It was at this point that I decided to study myself. I decided to start the study by considering myself first in any decision I wanted to make – provided that decision was not a sin, as I am a Christian and I believe in God. I started to practise deep self-love. I took extra care in doing things I would normally rush through, such as having my bath, getting dressed, singing and dancing, but now I did these same things with intention and purpose.

I went on a journey that I called YOUNIVERSITY: THE STUDY OF MYSELF. I ask you here, do you really know yourself? It's time you studied you so you can make better choices and decisions: this will benefit your life a great deal.

I wanted to get to know ME again and fall in love with ME. I started a journal about myself. I wrote so many things, such as what I really wanted out of life; where I would see myself in a year, five years, or ten years; what did I want to do that I hadn't done in the past; what did I like; and what did I dislike. I started to write things about Lady Edith Ebohon, including my best colour, my best Bible verse, my best song, my best hair style, my interests, my passions, my this, and my that. This helped me in developing a relationship with myself.

Another thing I did was to do what I would normally do for or with him for myself. For example, I took myself out on dates; I cooked nice meals for myself; I bought myself gifts; I took the time to look good for me. I changed things about me, such as having a new hair style or a new way of dressing.

Choose something pleasing to you. Remember that this is your life, and you owe no one any explanation about what you choose to do or not do. Answer this question now: 'What truly makes you happy?' If you cannot find the answer, then it is time to search deep within you. Once you find the answer, make that happiness come to life for you.

After doing these things, I could boldly rise if anyone asked, 'Would the real Lady Edith Ebohon stand up?' Because, now, I knew me again. Previously, I did not know me as I could no longer find 'me'.

Learn how to describe yourself: write it out. I spend time repeatedly finding myself, loving myself, discovering myself, and embracing myself. I recognise that I do not own myself, but that God owns me. I am his princess, his girl, his sweetheart, and he wants me to heal; he has me. He loves me; he cares for me. I gave up having a victim mentality; I engaged with my real self. There is more to me. My self-worth, self-identity, self-awareness, and self-development have improved. Your value is not your job, your role, your marital status, profession, beauty, what you own, and so on, but your value is in God. You are wonderfully made.

Another way I learned about myself was by doing various personality tests. These I found on the Internet, and I listened to many speakers on YouTube talk about them. The one that resonated the most with me was the test that says that there are four personality types: sanguine, choleric, melancholic, and pragmatic. After studying them,

I knew which I was. This is worth doing, as it will help you to understand why you do what you do and why you act in certain ways; it will improve your self-discovery.

The words you say to yourself.
Your internal conversation that no one hears.
The thoughts you think about you.
It all matters.

If you do not think that you are worthy, no one else will; if you do not love yourself, no one else will. You will just fall into the same trap of looking for happiness, validation, and affirmation from others when only you can truly validate yourself.

For example, if you say to yourself, 'I am no good. No one loves me. I amount to nothing,' then those are exactly the vibes you will project to others and you will always be treated that way.

Stop feeling you have lost; positively affirm yourself.
Learn and relearn to live again.
Be genuinely happy.
Do not compromise on your happiness – especially now, in the early days of being left alone.
See this season of your life as an opportunity to recover and rediscover who you really are and who God designed you to be.
God has given you this season as a gift.
This too can bring you closer to God. How do you want it?
This too can bring glory to God.
Ask him daily for his direction, for a strategy, for a road map, for a plan.

Poem 4

Delete

I woke up today and decided to delete the past.
But how do you delete the past – the happy times, the sad times?
How do you delete the moments of joy and happiness?
The church times; the praying-together times;
the nights out; the pictures; date nights; movie nights;
the meals we ate, cooking together.
Dancing together; going out with friends.
Laughing and joking and partying;
making up after a fight; the bed we shared.
The sex, the cuddling, and hugs;
the travel and holidays.
How do you delete the memories of years of being together?
How do you delete the smiles he put on my face, or the tears he made me cry;
the way he made me smile and held my hands?
How do you delete the plans for the future?
How can you stop thinking about the promise of eternity you made to each other?
How do you go on without remembering your wedding vows?
How do you even begin to delete and let go of so much?
But then I said, 'He made a choice to go.
He decided for whatever reason to leave.'
I wanted to spend my life with him and build a beautiful empire, but he left.
He is gone, so delete I must.
I faced my truth and reality: I am alone.
I realise that I must make decisions for my comfort and safety.
It's just me now. He left.

I know I do not feel like letting go because everything is way tooooooo heavy: too difficult.
It's like a movie. It looks and feels so unreal.
Is he on holiday or just out of the home?
No! He is out of my life. He left.
I was not ready to be ready for this.
I have been stressing.
But it's time to let go.
It's time to delete.
And it is okay to delete because my blessings are on the way.
I am not worried about what they say. They say. Let them say!
For me, he is gone.
He left, so it's time to delete.
I AM DELETING. IT IS A PROCESS. I WILL COMPLETE IT.
I AM STRONG.
I will heal. I will live again. I must live again.
Jesus has got me.

Chapter Four

Dealing with losses

One day, I woke up and I realised that being left alone was not actually new to me. I do not mean the time of my widowhood but from my childhood.

I was left alone on my first day at a boarding school. As an 11-year-old, I knew no one in Federal Government Girls' College, Benin City, Edo State, Nigeria.

I was left alone the day I came to the United Kingdom. I was sent by my mum and dad to further my education at the age of 18.

I felt left alone when my mum passed away; I felt I had lost my covering.

I was left alone at that crucial moment when I was about to commit suicide, because I felt worthless, useless, and a failure after my first husband passed away. I did not know how to continue with my life or care for my two children.

I was left alone on my first day in a new job, when I was supposed to be leading a team of eight but there was only one other individual. I had to do the work of all the team members myself at various times. I had to devise new ways to recruit staff, reduce the waiting list, and make the team I was leading work.

Yes, being left alone was familiar territory for me. But this one hit differently: my love left.

Some other losses I have encountered that many might also relate to include those regarding material possessions, dreams and visions, health, identity, roles, abuse, and so on.

Basically, when I thought about my being left alone, I realised that I had been going through life not even knowing that I'd had so many losses and 'left alone moments'. The beauty of it all is that losses and 'left-alone times' shape and beautify one's life. Please do not run away from dealing with your losses.

The key is to understand where you lost yourself so you can find yourself . . . again.

I decided to attend therapy. There is a lot of choice out there but, for me, I felt that Christian therapy was what I needed. For me, no GOD: no ME. I was introduced to a Christian ladies' group soon after I was left alone; there, the answer to my quest to deal with my losses came. The ladies ran a therapy group called Regain.

The aim of Regain is to find yourself again. It is to meet others like you whom you can support, and who can support you. It is to hear the word of God and learn new things about yourself. It is just like when you are trying to complete a jigsaw puzzle and you cannot because one or two pieces of the puzzle are missing: the result is you cannot see the full, beautiful picture of the puzzle. Regain helped me to find the two or three missing pieces in my life, which, in turn, helped me on my journey of self-discovery and healing.

The first session of the programme started with each participant writing out their losses. I was amazed at how much I had lost. My losses, from childhood to teenage years to adulthood, were a lot. No wonder my life was so broken. I had been going through losses over and over and over again, with no healing. I was however comforted by the word of God, which was an intrinsic part of the sessions. The negative impacts of losses in the past lead to so much that might have an effect on the rest of one's life. For example, they might lead to masking pain, negative decision-making, and losing one's identity and authentic self.

It is important to know what is lost in order to know what needs to be recovered and regained. Loss of any kind has an impact that affects one's self-worth. It is only God, in my humble opinion, who can take one back to the place of loss to begin the journey of healing. This is vital because many go through life without even knowing that something is missing or lost. They will never be able to fulfil their full potential and the life of purpose God has called them to.

What exactly does it mean to me to REGAIN? To 'regain' anything implies to restore or regain ownership of it, control of it, or a prior state or condition of it after having lost it, not having it, or having it decreased in some way. After suffering a loss, a setback, or a decline, the term 'regain' refers to the process of going back to or returning to a prior condition or level. It is applicable to many facets of life, including one's health, strength, self-assurance, abilities, relationships, or power, to name a few. In most cases, regaining anything requires making an effort or going through a procedure in order to bring back what was lost, or to replace what was absent.

The Regain programme was able to support me to understand a few things:

What my losses were.
What the concept and process of recovery and resilience are.
It acknowledged that setbacks and losses are an inevitable part of life, but that they are not necessarily permanent.
It enabled us, the participants, to recognise the potential for growth, development, and positive change when we regained something.
It emphasised the possibility of reclaiming what was lost, repairing what was damaged, and overcoming any obstacles that impeded our progress.
It enabled me to understand that regaining can inspire hope, motivate action, and serve as a reminder of our inner fortitude and resiliency.

It emphasised the significance of perseverance, tenacity, and learning from past experiences to move forward and recover what we value or aspire to attain.

It convinced me, through numerous biblical examples, that God was with me; he loved me and he would restore me.

The Regain programme was one of the main events that caused a pivotal change in my life, and I wholeheartedly endorse it. After finishing the course, I was able to create new progress and success in my life, and my testimonies were great because I had discovered myself. This was all because I had completed the therapy.

Do you desire and yearn to be who God has called you to be?

Do you want to live a life that fulfils the purpose of God in your life?

Do you seek to regain what has been lost in your life?

Then you need the Regain programme.

Please get in touch with me if you are interested in taking Regain.

Poem 5

Life is one big fight

I always knew that life is a battleground, and you must fight to win.
I always knew that I had to fight, and I did fight.
But it came to a day when I felt drained of energy and was tired of fighting.
I was about to give up, but then I said, 'No, no, no! I will not talk defeat to myself. I will not allow what someone else has done to me make me give up.'
So, I decided to fight.
I started my fight by letting go of everything: every hurt, every pain, every disappointment, everything that has ever had a hold on me.
I decided that I was not going to be scared or hide away because of my hurt,
but to stand tall and be strong.
I forgave them.
I wished them the best.
I stopped focusing on them.
I decided to focus on me.
I gave my all.
I invested a lot.
So, I still felt hurt; the pain was still so raw.
But I realised that there were happy times, and there was no amount I could pay for my happiness. So I took all my investments and sacrifice to be a payment for the happy times.
That helped me to let go.
I then stopped caring about the past and what people said or thought.
For me now, it's 'Whatever! You think and say what you like!'

If you feel that I made a mistake or you judge me or say negative things about me, so be it. All it means to me is that you do not want me to do better in life; so, if I am aware of that, I delete you.
I unsubscribe from all your issues.
Otherwise, all you will do is be negative and get me down. And I do not want that.
Why? Because
no pain is for ever.
It is hard for me to forget what happened to me, how my life has been, all the twists and turns. But, hey, it is a new day.
I know that God is still with me.
Life is one big fight,
every day and every night.
Yet I am going to be all right;
I am going to do well.
Life can be cruel; life can be hard,
but I have got to keep fighting.
I cannot let down my guard.
The battles I have been through make me who I am.
I had to learn how to be proud of my scars.

Chapter Five

Support

Having a support network is something that I cannot overemphasise as a requirement for anyone who is going through, or has just been through, a hard time. It is crucial for your well-being and recovery. A support network consists of a group of individuals who provide emotional, practical, and, sometimes, financial assistance. Typically, these individuals or groups are friends, family members, co-workers, or professionals who are willing to offer assistance and encouragement during difficult times or significant life events.

At that time of low mood and pain, I used my support network. I already had people I knew loved and cared about me before my loss started. I would call them to rant, vent, cry, just talk, pray with me, hug me, advise me – basically for anything I needed. I knew who was good at what, and I knew whom I should to call for whichever need I had.

It is important to have different sets of people for support: for example, a prayer partner to pray with you for strength and peace; a coach to lead you in the next steps; a critical friend to tell you the bitter truth and open your eyes to what you are not seeing (and I tell you, at such low times, one might make a very unwise decision, therefore a critical friend is important); and, of course, someone you can rant and vent to, who will just listen and absorb the pain you need to let out.

There are other benefits I found that I was able to get from my different sources of support. Before I list them, I want to say here that GOD was my biggest source of support. I found out that the days I prayed more and connected with God in silence, meditated on scriptures, and listened to Bible teachings were days I was calmer and able to deal with my pain.

I would literally spend hours writing out Bible chapters, especially at night, when I could not sleep and the pain of emptiness was great. At such times, I found deep solace in God's words. The silence of the night would engulf me, with warmth from the throne above. After all, he said I should come to him when I am weak for, there, I would find peace.

My network helped me with emotional support: it provided empathy, understanding, and a safe space to express my feelings and emotions. My friends would listen to me without judgment, offer a shoulder to lean on, and provide comfort whenever I needed it. My network also offered practical support, such as helping with daily tasks, offering advice, sharing their experiences, or providing guidance in specific areas. They helped me brainstorm solutions, they offered resources, and aided me in accomplishing various goals.

The beauty of having a diverse support network is that you get different perspectives on issues, which can broaden your understanding of a situation. A variety of people can provide alternative viewpoints, challenge your assumptions, and help you to consider different options when making decisions. After which, you need to find time to sit and critically think about what you need to do. At every stage, make sure you put God first and yourself next. Go all out to be happy because you deserve to be.

Friends in a good support network also act as cheerleaders. They can provide encouragement and motivation when you face challenges or pursue your goals. They believe in your abilities and provide the extra push needed to keep you motivated and focused. They ensure you have a sense of belonging and connectedness. They provide opportunities for social interaction, companionship, and can help to reduce feelings of isolation or loneliness.

However, there might be times when you feel that you do not know how to seek support. This was one thing I learned: I needed to seek support to reduce burnout and the feeling of being overwhelmed. I learned to contact my loved ones, those I trusted, to share my experiences and my feelings. They gave me emotional support and a listening ear. They offered comfort and understanding.

I also looked for and joined support groups that addressed my needs and the challenges I was facing. Many of these were online and on social-media platforms, so it was easy to connect and take part in their activities. I learned so much that helped me on my journey of recovery. Connecting with others who have gone through similar experiences can provide a sense of validation, understanding, and mutual support.

It was important for me to prioritise my self-care, and I recommend this point to you: make sure that you prioritise your self-care. It is so easy to let yourself go and not look good when going through a difficult time in life. Engage in self-care activities that promote your well-being. This can include getting enough restful sleep, maintaining a healthy diet, exercising regularly, practising relaxation techniques, and engaging in activities that bring you joy and help you to unwind.

One other point I want to make here is that, when you go out and mix, you will find that others are living their lives despite your pain, and you must come to terms with this. You used to hold and hug your beau in public, so now you must watch others do it, too. Do not be sad when others talk about their positive experience in marriage. Do not be jealous.

Remember, seeking support is a sign of strength, and you don't have to face difficult times alone. Different support options work for different individuals, so explore what feels most comfortable and effective for you. It's important to reach out and ask for help when you need it, as support can make a significant difference to your healing and recovery process.

I also want to add here that there is a place for support that you can draw from yourself: you need to be resilient. You draw support from yourself by thinking, and critically thinking some more, about what you need to do and what is best for you. You need to actually deal with the past by meditating and thinking about what you did wrong or right, how you contributed to the break-up and what lessons you learned from the experience. I suggest you journal about it. It was at these times that I was able to write my poems; they helped me a lot when I read them again.

Reflection is also a good way to put things into perspective. Look within and begin to ask God to help you.

Poem 6

The scars

I have some scars:
some deep-rooted scars.
These scars are in my heart; they are in my mind; and they are in my emotions.
They have been caused by the one I allowed to make them because I trusted them.
They left me pained, shaken, broken, and caused scars and marks in me.
But, today, I choose to celebrate that I am proud of my scars.
The scars show me that I am still alive.
The pain shows me that I am a fighter.
The brokenness shows me that I overcame.
It means I went through it; I have faith and I am using it to birth the person that I want to be; the woman God created me to be.
I will not let my past affect my today and my future.
I will look at my scars, celebrate them and move on.
I cannot allow my hurt to ruin where I am now.
I have washed my past off so I can move forward.
I am not defined by my past, as it stops opportunities for my today.
I have a fresh attitude.
I am a different kind of woman.
I am a WOW woman.

Chapter Six

Mood pickers

While it is normal and natural to experience a range of emotions, it is important to be mindful of our mood and take steps to maintain a balanced and positive state whenever possible. It's important to note that experiencing occasional low moods is a normal part of life; but if low mood becomes persistent, interferes with daily functioning, or is accompanied by other symptoms, it may be helpful to seek professional help to address underlying concerns.

Maintaining a positive mood and mental well-being is essential for everyone for a variety of reasons. First and foremost, regardless of the circumstances or situations we are facing, we must remember that our mood has a big influence on our entire mental health and well-being. We must give our mood, emotions, and feelings to God as only he can support us to be truly happy. The peace we seek comes only from God and it is permanent. When we are in a good mood, we have more resilience, better coping abilities, and higher mental functioning. We can make better decisions; we can hear from God; we can do positive things. It can also help us to deal with stress and adjust to life's obstacles.

You must do what makes you happy and have a positive mood, which is something only you can determine for yourself.

Second, studies have revealed a substantial correlation between our mood and our physical well-being. Chronic negative moods, such as extended sorrow or depression, have been linked to an increased risk of a variety of physical health concerns, including heart disease, a weaker immune system, and digestive disorders. Positive emotions, on the other hand, have been linked to improved physical health and a stronger immune system.

Third, our mood may have a significant impact on how we connect with people and the quality of our relationships. When we are in a good mood, we are more accessible, engaged, and empathetic, which leads to better interactions with people. Negative emotions, on the other hand, can damage relationships and lead to social isolation.

Fourth, positive emotions can improve our cognition, creativity, and productivity. When we are in a good mood, we are more focused, motivated, and able to complete activities quickly. This may have a favourable influence on many aspects of life, including work, academic studies, and personal objectives. We need to be creative at these times and find things that will make us successful. This book was born out of such low moments: I was able to be creative because I focused on having positive emotions.

Finally, our mood has a large impact on our total sense of happiness, fulfilment, and life satisfaction. Positive moods increase our likelihood of enjoying and appreciating life's events, engaging in important activities, and having a better feeling of purpose and fulfilment.

I used my personal experience whilst going through the time I was left alone. I was lonely, sad and low in mood; as I gradually healed, I knew I needed inspiration. I needed to fill that void/space and I needed to know what would work for me to achieve this. I was very aware that my emotions were up and down, and it showed in my interactions with others, my behaviour, and my decision-making. I might be happy at one time and then be sad within a few hours. I was like a yoyo (lol), and this needed to change. In 1 Samuel 30:6–8, we see how David encouraged himself in the Lord. Those verses inspired me to begin to work on myself and encourage myself; that ability had to come from within me, with the help of God.

I've listed here the steps that I took to make sure I regained complete control over my emotions.

Noticing my emotions: I became more in touch with my emotions. I began to notice when I was starting to feel low, which might have come from a trigger: for example, remembering a past event or my emotional pain; the trigger might even have been a film or a conversation – anything – but I was able to recognise this when it happened.

Praying: this became a pattern for me. I would pray as soon as I started to feel low. I would pray when I showered, when I was dressing, when I was driving, and at any given opportunity. I would sometimes pray silently; at other times, loudly. I would sing worship songs, when I was unable to pray, or I would recite psalms. My favourite psalms are Psalms 1, 23, 27, 34, 121 and 130. These greatly helped me to divert my attention from my negative thoughts.

Diverting my attention: for the first time in my life, I spent a great amount of time thinking and rethinking. I thought about what I did wrong, what I could do better now, and what I wanted to achieve.

Putting my thoughts down: I wrote everything I was thinking down; and if I was unable to write, I would record a voice memo on my phone. Journalling is a great form of self-therapy. It was good for me, as I was able to release my emotions. Sometimes I cried; sometimes I shouted; sometimes I spoke to God, or pretended to be advising myself or someone else. Today, I read my notes or listen to the voice memos, and I feel so empowered when I think of how far I have come.

Engaging in activities I enjoy: I did activities that bring me joy and pleasure. This included my hobbies, such as listening to music, watching my favourite movie or TV show, reading a book, going for a walk in nature, or spending time with loved ones. I alo9s learnt new skills, I read the Bible, decluttered my wardrobe, and rearranged my home: there are so many things I did, get creative!

Expressing gratitude: I focused on the positive aspects of my life and practised gratitude. I took time to appreciate the things I am grateful for, whether it's small moments of joy, supportive relationships, or personal achievements. I kept a gratitude journal in which I jotted down things I am thankful for each day.

Challenging negative thoughts: negative thoughts can contribute to low mood. Therefore, I tried to identify negative thought patterns and challenge them by replacing them with more positive or realistic thoughts.

Engaging in physical activity: physical activity has been shown to boost mood and release endorphins, which are natural mood-lifting chemicals in the brain. I engaged in exercise I enjoyed, such as going for a run, zumba, dancing, or participating in a team sport.

Remember that everyone's experience is unique, and different strategies may work better for different individuals. It may take some trial and error to find the techniques that work best for you. If you continue to struggle with a persistently low mood, it is important to consult with a health-care professional for a comprehensive evaluation and personalised recommendations. It was during this time that I learned I could never be bored, and that helped me during the pandemic lockdowns, when we all had to stay indoors. It was then that I wrote my first book, *Life's Golden Gems*.

Caveat: you cannot be happy always, so you need to develop a spirit of resilience to go through life.

Poem 7

My identity in Christ

I am first a child of God, a woman of God, before I am a mother or a wife or anything else. I am defined by who made me and for what purpose, and not by my title or my role in life. I am not defined by being a wife or a mother, or by my career or job title or by what I earn, where I live or what I drive; those things come to me as gifts because I am a child of God.

As a result, I am –
ENOUGH, COMPLETE, and WHOLE.
I am not what my culture or what society or even the church says I am.
Nobody in the whole world is like me.
I have been abused, used, betrayed, and suffered many challenges, including in health and marriage.
I have moved from being a single lady to being married, then a widow; then, because of widowhood, becoming a single mother and remarrying again, and now divorced. And then I ask, 'GOD WHY?'
I am not saying, 'WHY ME?' I am saying, 'WHY?' There is a big difference!!!
'Why me?' means I am pitying myself.
'Why me?' means I think God made a mistake.
'Why me?' is saying, 'Look at you. You are no good!'
'Why me?' is from the pit of hell.
But 'Why?' is saying, 'God, what is it you are teaching me? Where are you taking me to? What am I supposed to do with this experience?' and many questions like that.
We have been taught to seek identity in social media, relationships, career, kids, money, books, and magazines; through spiritual leaders or through our husbands. We

seek identity everywhere but in Jesus Christ, the author and creator of our identity.

Chapter Seven

Find your purpose

One day, I went to my pastor; I asked him why bad thing happens to good people or to children of God. I am not saying that I am a good person, but I believe, to a large extent, I do not do bad things to others.

We spoke for a long time that day, and I learned so much about myself. In summary, what I learned was that there is no straightforward answer to this question of why bad things happen to good people. But, when you begin to think about it, you will get your answer and the answer will make you realise your purpose. I believe the way to move on when you are in a fix is to find your purpose.

The rationale or inspiration for someone's actions, decisions, or the existence of anything is typically referred to as its purpose. What we do has significance and direction because of the underlying objective or intention. The only way to find your purpose is to seek it from God.

Finding your purpose and where you fit in God's plan is a process that is both unique and continuous. It is essential to approach this with an open heart, a willingness to learn, and a strong feeling of reverence for the spiritual path you are on to be successful. Finding one's purpose frequently entails determining what provides fulfilment, satisfaction, and a feeling of significance in life.

Purpose is the underlying reason for your existence. It is about identifying why you exist, what you want to achieve, and how to contribute positively to society. There is one thing I know: God has no time to make a nobody; everyone has something to give. Purpose will provide direction, lead decision-making, and provide drive and fulfilment. It is frequently connected with a sense of enthusiasm, involvement, and alignment between the values, aims, and activities of an individual.

When you have a strong sense of purpose, it may have a significant influence on many elements of your life. You have a better sense of what is actually important to you and where you want to direct your time and energy. You wake up excited because you're involved in activities and interests that correspond with your basic beliefs and objectives. You have the sense that your life has value and that you are contributing to something bigger than yourself. Your sense of purpose gives you the determination to continue in the face of adversity.

Knowing and living one's purpose in a spiritual context can lead to a strong sense of connection with the divine and a better comprehension of one's spiritual path. Living out your mission can help you to leave a legacy. Even after you've gone, your effect and influence might continue to inspire others.

I dare say that it was finding my purpose that ultimately led me to come out of being alone and to begin to walk the path that had been chosen for me. There is nothing I can do about the past and what has happened, but there is a lot I can do about what will happen next in my life.

In my case, I was blessed with an idea of what God created me for. I knew my purpose. I now had to begin to live my purpose, deploy it, and succeed in it. As I started to do so, I found a great sense of satisfaction and fulfilment. Spending time living my dreams meant that I had time to think about my issues.

I wrote out my goals and worked towards achieving them. They included aims for my health, my family, and my spiritual walk with God; and also my ministry, career, work, education, social life, and so much more. I aligned myself with God's words and intentions for me in the realms of prayer, mentorship, and reflection.

I explored my passions: what I loved to do and always wanted to do but was never able to do. I started travelling the world and dressing the way I wanted to. I pursued hobbies, such as writing, crocheting, learning new recipes, and other interests that energised and inspired me. This helped me to identify my values and what was important to me. I also reflected on my strengths. I took inventory of my talents, skills, and strengths. I considered how I could use these gifts to contribute to others and to the world around me.

At this point, I had great testimonies; I paid off my debts; I began my YouTube show, *Relationship Tips, Talks and Tales*. I wrote my first book, *Life's Golden Gems*, which was taken from my other You tube show, *Two Minute Sunday*. I began to excel at my career. I started a master's programme. There was a new me emerging.

Even though I was a person who had suddenly lost her home, spouse, role, activities, togetherness, and intimacy, I realised that I had not lost GOD; I had not lost life. There was still so much to live for. I realised that I was made to be a person that would use my stories to inspire and empower others. God is a God who never fails. The road is rough; it is painful, but – hey – you can still rise above it all.

Look at these scriptures from the New Living Translation of the Bible:

'For we are God's masterpiece. He has created us anew in Christ Jesus, so we can do the good things he planned for us long ago.' (Ephesians 2:10)

'And I am certain that God, who began the good work within you, will continue his work until it is finally finished on the day when Christ Jesus returns.' (Philippians 1:6)

Yes, God made me with a purpose.

I have something else to talk about. Even though I was feeling stronger and better, I would still get some thoughts that lingered for many months.

How do you feel when something great that has happened to you – which you were congratulated for, and which gave you joy and happiness – is suddenly no longer there?

How do you start to explain to others what has happened – that the person has left? People will ask. I got to the stage that, when people asked me about my husband, I lied that he was fine. I got tired of explaining (or pretending) that we were still together. So, I decided to own up to the truth and, when I was asked, I would simply say that we were both fine but no longer together. I got various reactions, as you can imagine. However, this started to liberate me and I began to feel whole. The important thing was that we actually were both fine. We still spoke now and again; we were not enemies. I have no time to make anyone my enemy. God hates that.

God created you uniquely. You have your own strengths, personality, and potential. But do you know what they are?

Do not focus on the things that make you feel unloved and inadequate.

Walk past them!

There is a place for authenticity.

No need to lie.

No need to make excuses but, ultimately, be wise about whom you talk to

Some people are not genuinely sympathetic; they just want to hear your gist.

Do not bother.

Remember: focus on your purpose!

Poem 8

I have let go . . .

I have let go. I had to.
It is time for me to say goodbye.
It is time for me to let you go because you have completed your purpose in my life.

I am picking up the pieces.
I have a void in my heart.
I remember all the promises and all the beautiful memories we shared together,
but you, my ex, have chosen to move on, and I must accept your decision.
I do not want you back because you lie; you walked away and you undermined me.
So it's best you left.
I am now single and alone, and I am discovering myself and looking hard at myself: becoming who God wants me to be
In fact, thanks for leaving.
Thanks for freeing me to embrace true happiness.
Thanks for being bold and confident to damn all consequences, and choose what you really felt was best for you.
I thought I would be afraid to be alone.
I thought I would die.
But no. Today, I have power.
I am free.
I am no more a prisoner.

Chapter Eight

King and queen

After finding out your purpose, it is time to live as the queen or king that you are. Becoming a king or a queen is important before you even think of becoming a wife or a husband again. You must heal and be whole. Do not be desperate to enter a new relationship or marriage, but rather work on yourself.

Marriage is not a prerequisite to making heaven. Have boundaries and standards. Boundaries and standards are two important concepts in maintaining healthy relationships and self-care. Set them up before you meet someone new.

Boundaries refer to the limits you set on what you are willing to tolerate from others. They can be physical, emotional, or social; they help you to communicate your needs and protect your well-being. Examples of boundaries can include saying 'no' to requests that you are uncomfortable with, taking time for yourself when you need it, and communicating your feelings in a respectful way.

Standards refer to the qualities and values that you look for in yourself and others. They are the criteria you use to judge whether someone is a good match for you or not. Examples of standards can include honesty, trust, respect, and communication.

Keeping healthy boundaries and standards can help you to establish and maintain sound relationships with others, and to take care of yourself. Here are some tips for setting and maintaining healthy boundaries and standards:

How does a king or queen live? I see myself as a queen, a lady, and God's special daughter. I am an energy goddess, a happiness minister, a vibe queen, and much more. I see myself in a new light.

A king or queen lives in a palace. Start by making your home your palace: your happy place, your sanctuary. Decorate it the way you want. Live a nice life of making sure you do what makes you happy.

A king or queen will adorn themselves with beautiful things, so make sure you do same. Note that I did not say expensive things but beautiful things that you like. You do not need to get into debt or spend a lot to look clean and beautiful, and smell good. Do you for once, and be you.

Marriage is healthy and can be sweet. Do not let the bad experience you had make you run from trying again. Trust God and tread with caution.

What exactly are you looking for in the opposite sex?

Remember that you are a new you, you have come out strong, bold and you are ready to live like the queen or king that you really are.

Be ready for others to want to rain on your parade or to remind you of your past.

Get ready for when the negatives occur or the disappointments happen.

A king or queen always rules in their kingdom, so be ready to be resilient and face that challenge, and win over and over and over again.

Poem 9

My happiness

I am living purposefully a life pleasing to the Lord.

I am able to praise him in the midst of pain and also in good times.
I cannot afford to be a spectator in my life.
As a result, I am creating my own happiness.
My happiness is about me.
My happiness is about what God wants for me.

It is not about what society expects, what the church says, what friends think, or what the government dictates.
No one can put me in a box.
My happiness is about ME. I repeat: my happiness is about me.
My happiness is about not expecting anything from any man. If I get anything, it is a gift and God made it so.
My happiness is about realising that God made me and he made me with intention.
My happiness is to find that intention and live it.
My happiness is to choose daily what I want, based on God's plans for me.

Chapter Nine

Finding love again

Finding love again, after a relationship ends, is a personal and unique journey for everyone. Some people decide to remain single for ever; some decide to remain single for a while; and some decide to go into another relationship soon afterwards. Based on my own experience, I would suggest that, after a relationship breakdown, one needs time to heal and recover. I would not advise you to go into another relationship immediately. Wounds need time to heal.

This is important for many reasons. Break-ups can be emotionally difficult and necessitate time for healing and processing the emotions associated with the end of a relationship. Jumping into another relationship too rapidly can prevent you from completely processing your emotions and may result in the transfer of unresolved emotional baggage into the new relationship. A period of introspection enables you to contemplate the dynamics of your previous relationship, comprehend your role in it, and identify any patterns or opportunities for personal development. Spending time on oneself can result in increased self-awareness, self-discovery, and personal growth. A relationship breakdown, separation, or divorce can sometimes leave one feeling wounded, spurned, or insecure. Spending time on self-care, self-love, and restoring your self-esteem can help you to regain confidence, and ensure that you enter your next relationship from a position of strength and self-assurance.

There is something I consider quite dangerous that happens in society, both to ladies and gentlemen, and that is going into another relationship without healing. Doing that means you are using the new person on the 'rebound'. Rebound relationships occur when, after a break-up, an individual initiates a new relationship briefly without addressing their emotional needs or entirely healing. These relationships may not be founded on genuine compatibility or a firm foundation, which may lead to complications and additional sorrow. Taking a break from dating gives you the opportunity to define your own needs, set personal limits, and decide what you want in a future relationship. It allows you to focus on your own objectives, hobbies, and interests without jeopardising your sense of self.

However, the time that it takes for someone to heal varies from individual to individual. There is no set time-frame, but received wisdom suggests that the longer you were in a relationship, the longer it will take you to heal. Additionally, if you invested a lot in that relationship the healing might take longer. It is vital to understand that there is no set schedule for progress, and it may be a slow process. Allow yourself the time and space you need to recover, and find yourself before embarking on a new relationship. Before going on a new love adventure, trust your instincts and make sure you are truly ready and emotionally open.

Next, I want to discuss some suggestions that I found helpful.

I allowed myself time and space to heal. I reflected on what I learned from the experience, and I focused on self-care. I thought about what I wanted in a relationship. I considered my values, goals, and the knowledge that I had now learnt about myself. During this period of opening my mind to find love again, I focused on my personal growth and self-improvement so that I could be properly ready for this new journey.

However, there was a part of me that said, 'Is it worth going into another relationship at all? Why can't I just remain single?' I had so many moments of doubt. I found that when someone chatted me up, I became very critical of them. I made remarks such as 'Marriage is a scam, born from a place of pain and hurt.' This comment indicated a negative perspective on marriage, implying that it is fundamentally misleading and stems from unpleasant feelings. It's vital to recognise that people's attitudes about marriage can vary greatly. While some people have terrible experiences or ideas about marriage, many others find it to be a rewarding and significant institution.

Marriage is a complicated and highly personal commitment that may provide partners with pleasure, love, friendship, and personal progress. It establishes a legal and sociological framework for the acknowledgement of the tie between partners, as well as a basis for establishing a life together. Many people enter into marriage with good intentions, hoping for a lasting relationship built on trust, love, and shared ideals. However, it is important to recognise that not all marriages are successful, and some people may have had unpleasant experiences that have influenced their image of marriage. It is critical to appreciate different points of view and recognise that people's attitudes to marriage can be shaped by their individual circumstances and personal experiences.

Therefore, my opinion is that it is healthy to look for love again, should you so desire. Remember that finding love is a process, and it's okay to take things slowly and go at your own pace. Stay positive and keep an open mind, and you may find love when you least expect it. You need to understand that God is love and love is from God, and be guided by this when finding love. I dare say that anyone who does not love God will not know love, and will find it hard to give love to anyone else. I also dare say that anyone who does not love themselves cannot love another, as you cannot give what you don't have.

No matter how sweet the love is between you and anyone else, if it is not of GOD, it will end in pain. Ask God to help you choose. The relationship might have challenges, and things might not look right, but if it has the hand of God on it, these challenges will pass. Remember that all that glitters is not gold, and all that seems good might not be from God.

And, yes, my story ends here . . . I found love again.

Closing remarks

Let the new you come out. Here I am.

I have new ways I describe myself these days because I now know who I am, and I appreciate all my wounds, pains, and the healing period. My wounds are now scars that make me different and beautiful.

'Let the new me come out' is a phrase that suggests embracing change and allowing oneself to grow and evolve. It can be a reminder to let go of past habits, beliefs, and behaviours that no longer serve you, and to embrace new experiences and opportunities that allow you to become the best version of yourself.

To let the new you come out, it's important to be open to new experiences, to challenge yourself to try new things, and to embrace change as a natural part of life. This can involve setting goals, learning new skills, exploring different hobbies, or making new connections with people who share your interests and values.

It's also important to practise self-compassion and to be patient with yourself as you navigate the process of change. Remember that personal growth is a journey, and it takes time and effort to develop new habits and ways of thinking. Celebrate your progress along the way, and don't be afraid to ask for support from others when you need it.

It is possible to win and be alive again even after you have been left alone. God wants to talk to you and reveal to you his reason for creating you; he will whisper in your ear. Please just dedicate your life to him.

>There is more to you.
>You are complete.
>You are whole.

All you did was love the wrong person, and you have paid the price for this.

So it is time to LET THE NEW YOU LIVE AGAIN.

Enjoy!

I Am Alone: What Next?

Our world can seem consumed by solitude and sad times, but there can also be happy occasions; and there is always a solution to a difficulty. I found myself in a place where the echoes of human existence became faint. My extraordinary voyage took me to somewhere I found myself alone. This can happen to many other people, too, for various reasons.

I Am Alone: What Next? is a book that examines the resilience of the human spirit in the face of desolation. It delves deeply into the heart of solitude, where grace and hope can meet to bring a solution from the almighty Father.

The book tells the tale of how the writer was left alone but overcame. It gives insights and ideas on how others who have been left alone can do same. Weighed down by the burden of her solitary existence, she had to confront the overwhelming desolation that surrounded her.

Haunted by memories of a bygone era of love and unity in relationship, the writer embarked on an introspective quest to rediscover her purpose and forge a new path forwards. With each step, she encountered remnants of being left alone in the past that had always been there – a stark reminder of what was lost. Yet, amidst the desolation, glimmers of hope emerged, challenging the notion of her complete isolation: after all, God exists and is the way maker.

I Am Alone: What Next? explores themes of loneliness, resilience, and the indomitable human spirit. It paints a poignant picture of an individual's struggle to find meaning in a world devoid of connection. Through encounters with enigmatic characters and unforeseen challenges, the writer unravels the depths of her own inner strength, offering a beacon of hope in the darkest of times.

I Am Alone: What Next? is a thought-provoking and emotionally charged tale that will leave readers contemplating the true nature of human connection and the resilience of the human spirit. In the face of overwhelming isolation, one question remains: what comes after loneliness?

www.ingramcontent.com/pod-product-compliance
Lightning Source LLC
Chambersburg PA
CBHW070337120526
44590CB00017B/2926